CLASSIC RECIPES

Italian cooking

simple and delicious food

Wendy Hobson

ARCTURUS

ARCTURUS

This edition published in 2013 by Arcturus Publishing Limited
26/27 Bickels Yard, 151–153 Bermondsey Street,
London SE1 3HA

ISBN: 978-1-78212-011-7
AD002570US

Printed in China

Contents

Introduction 6

Melon with prosciutto 7

Insalata caprese 8

Eggplant, bell pepper, and zucchini with rosemary 9

Seafood linguine 10

Pasta puttanesca 11

Stuffed calamari 12

Garlic pizza with arugula and olives 14

Bacon-wrapped chicken 15

Chicken cacciatore 16

Breaded pork with lemon 17

Lasagne 18

Spaghetti and meatballs 20

Fried risotto balls 21

Potato gnocchi with tomato sauce 22

Wild mushroom risotto 23

Italian braised beef 25

Baked vegetable pasta 26

Chicken and olive pasta 27

Tiramisù 28

Cantuccini biscotti 29

Panna cotta 30

Notes and conversions 31

Italian style

The essence of Italian cookery is simplicity. Fresh, high-quality ingredients are selected for flavor, texture and color, then prepared with minimum fuss, cooked to bring out their finest textures and tastes, and given a piquancy with those familiar Mediterranean herbs. It is the perfect cuisine for our modern lifestyle.

Italian cooking is inclusive—a real family affair; everyone enjoys being involved in making the meal and sitting down together to eat, to talk, to laugh, and to enjoy the company of family and friends. Eating is a social occasion, whether it is a family supper at the end of the day or a special occasion when the whole extended family gets together.

A lot of care goes into choosing the freshest ingredients, so when you are cooking Italian-style, be prepared to be flexible. If you spot some lovely fresh arugula at the market, buy it and adapt your plans around what's fresh and in season. Bring home your produce and decide how best to cook it to release its wonderful textures and flavors.

Italian cooking involves some superb, rich sauces, but they never smother the flavors of the main ingredient—they bring out all the nuances of flavor so that everything blends together beautifully. And when you choose a dish that is cooked long and slow, it thickens and becomes rich all on its own—so there's no need to resort to cornstarch to give the sauce some substance.

Color and presentation are crucial. Think of the vibrant contrast of the red, green and white of the Italian flag and bring that into your ingredient selection. The classic insalata caprese demonstrates how simplicity can be stunning to look at—and to eat!

Though the special-occasion dishes take long, slow cooking, many Italian dishes are quick and easy to put together, so are ideal to make when you come home from a busy day at work. Keep a few staples in your storecupboard or freezer

and you'll always have the basis of a delicious Italian supper. They are:

- Onions
- Garlic
- Canned tomatoes
- Sieved tomatoes
- Frozen oregano and basil
- Pasta
- Risotto rice
- Olive oil
- Balsamic vinegar

Techniques are simple too so anyone can have a go. Children particularly enjoy making their own pizza and putting on just the right amount of their favorite toppings. It's cheaper and healthier than buying frozen or take-out pizzas, so why not give it a go and you'll soon wonder why you ever needed that take-out number by the phone!

Fresh herbs are also an integral part of Italian cooking, so grow some in your yard or have a few growing pots on your window sill. Basil, oregano, and rosemary are all must-haves! If you don't have room for fresh herbs, chop and freeze some if you can, or try the jars of herbs that keep in the fridge. They have a better flavor and texture than many dried herbs, although a jar of dried oregano in the cupboard will always come in handy.

The Mediterranean diet has been proved to be one of the healthiest, so bringing some Italian flavor into your diet is a good habit to get into. It's about following the principles we all know: plenty of fresh fruit and vegetables, moderate unrefined carbohydrates, a good mix of proteins, enough oil and fats but not too much (and olive oil is good), just a touch of sweetness as a treat—and enjoying a healthy variety and balance of foods.

This book will give you just a taster of some of the delights of Italian cooking. Hopefully it will inspire you to discover more and bring a ray of Italian sunshine into your kitchen.

Melon with prosciutto

Don't be put off by the simplicity of this classic Italian starter. The ripe, juicy melon is the perfect complement for the rich prosciutto and the combination is just substantial enough to whet the appetite without being too heavy. You can use any kind of melon, or try it with fresh figs too.

Serves 4

1 ogen or honeydew melon
A few handfuls of baby spinach leaves
8 slices of Italian ham (prosciutto crudo), halved
Freshly ground black pepper
A few chive stalks
3 tbsp olive oil
1½ tbsp balsamic vinegar
½ tsp mild mustard

1. Halve the melon and scoop out the seeds. Cut the flesh into crescents and cut off the rind.
2. Arrange the spinach leaves on serving plates.
3. Wrap the melon segments in the prosciutto and arrange them on the plates. Season with pepper and sprinkle with chives.
4. Whisk together the oil, balsamic vinegar, and mustard. Season to taste with pepper. Drizzle over the melon before serving. Any dressing left over can be kept in the fridge and used for salads.

Insalata caprese

With the tricolor of the Italian flag on the plate, there's no doubt diners are in Italian territory. Use buffalo mozzarella, if you can, for the ultimate flavor; it's more expensive but especially delicious. Take a little extra time to lay out the dish beautifully.

Serves 4

4 large ripe tomatoes, sliced
250g/9oz/2 balls buffalo mozzarella, sliced
A large sprig of fresh basil
Freshly ground black pepper
1 tsp balsamic vinegar
3 tbsp extra virgin olive oil
100g/4oz black olives (optional)

To serve
Ciabatta

1. Arrange the tomato and mozzarella slices alternately on serving plates, interleaving occasionally with a basil leaf.
2. Sprinkle generously with pepper.
3. Whisk the balsamic vinegar into the oil and drizzle over the salad.
4. Sprinkle with the olives, if liked, and serve with slices of ciabatta.

Eggplant, bell pepper, and zucchini with rosemary

This vegetable dish couldn't be easier to put together. If you prefer, you can cut the vegetables into smaller chunks to make cooking faster, but make sure you keep an eye on them so you can take them out of the oven when they are brown but not yet starting to burn.

Serves 4

120ml/4fl oz/½ cup olive oil
1 onion, halved or quartered
3 red onions, halved or quartered
Salt and freshly ground black pepper
A few rosemary sprigs
1 eggplant, thinly sliced lengthways
3 zucchini, thinly sliced lengthways
1 red bell pepper, cut into chunks
1 yellow bell pepper, cut into chunks

1. Heat the oven to 200°C/400°F/Gas 6.
2. Heat a large griddle pan over a high heat and drizzle with a little of the oil. When the oil is hot, add the onions and sauté for about 10 minutes until they are softened and just beginning to brown. Transfer to an ovenproof serving dish and season with salt and pepper. Strip the leaves off a rosemary sprig and sprinkle over the top.
3. Reduce the oven temperature to 180°C/350°F/Gas 4 and put the roasting pan in the oven while you cook the remaining vegetables.
4. Heat a little more oil in the griddle pan and sauté the eggplant for about 5 minutes each side until softened and nicely charred. Do not overcook as it will continue to cook in the oven. Put in the roasting pan with the onions.
5. Continue to cook the zucchini and peppers in the same way until all the vegetables are cooked. Keep an eye on the vegetables in the oven and turn down the oven temperature if they are beginning to brown to much.
6. When all the vegetables are ready, season to taste with salt and pepper, garnish with some fresh rosemary sprigs and serve.

Seafood linguine

Italians generally serve a robust pasta, such as conchiglie, with a dense sauce, but for lighter sauces, linguine or spaghetti are the perfect complement. Try this dish with different seafood options, adding any cooked seafood at the end to heat through.

Serves 4

800g/1¾lb clams in their shells, scrubbed
1 tsp grated lemon zest
120ml/4fl oz/½ cup white wine
Salt and freshly ground black pepper
400g/14oz linguine
2 tbsp olive oil
2 garlic cloves, crushed
4–8 cherry tomatoes, halved
2 tbsp vegetable stock
400g/14oz mixed seafood (optional)
2 tbsp chopped flatleaf parsley

1. Make sure the clams are thoroughly scrubbed and discard any that are open.
2. Place them in a large pan, add the lemon zest and wine, cover tightly and shake over a low heat for about 7 minutes until the clams have opened. Discard any that remain closed. Strain the liquid through a fine sieve and reserve.
3. Meanwhile, bring a large pan of salted water to the boil. Add the linguine and boil for about 7 minutes until it is *al dente*.
4. In a third pan, heat the oil and sauté the garlic gently for a few minutes until soft. Add the tomatoes and cook for 3 minutes.
5. Add the stock and reserved cooking liquor and warm through. Add the seafood, if using, and toss gently to coat in the sauce. Add the clams and linguine and toss together gently. Season with salt and pepper, and serve sprinkled with parsley.

Pasta puttanesca

Named for the ladies of the night, this simple dish of spaghetti in a rich and spicy tomato sauce laced with plenty of garlic, olives, and anchovies has become an international favorite. Adjust the paprika to taste or add chopped chili to the sauce if you like.

Serves 4

350g/12oz spaghetti
Salt and freshly ground black pepper
2 tbsp olive oil
4 garlic cloves, crushed
50g/2oz anchovies
200ml/7fl oz/scant 1 cup sieved tomatoes
1 tbsp capers
½ tsp paprika
A few basil sprigs
50g/2oz/½ cup stuffed olives, sliced
2 tomatoes, sliced

1. Bring a large pan of lightly salted water to the boil, add the spaghetti and boil for about 7 minutes until *al dente*.
2. Meanwhile, heat the oil in a large pan and sauté the garlic over a low heat for a few minutes to infuse the oil with the flavor.
3. Reserve a couple of anchovies for garnish and finely chop the remainder. Add to the pan with the sieved tomatoes, capers, and paprika and stir together.
4. Chop 1 tbsp of the basil and add it to the pan with the olives and tomatoes. Season to taste and stir gently until everything is hot and coated in the oil.
5. Drain the pasta, then add it to the pan and toss with the sauce. Serve garnished with the remaining anchovies and a few small basil sprigs.

Serves 4

2 tbsp oil

15g/½oz/1 tbsp butter

2 scallions, sliced into rings

1 red bell pepper, finely chopped

1 celery stick, finely chopped

1 garlic clove, chopped

200g/7oz/1 cup long-grain rice

200ml/7fl oz/scant 1 cup dry white wine

450ml/¾pt/2 cups vegetable or chicken stock

2 tbsp tomato paste

½ tsp cayenne

1 tbsp chopped parsley

Salt and freshly ground black pepper

8 calamari (squid) tubes

1 rosemary sprig

To serve

Hot Tomato Sauce (page 22)

Mixed salad

Stuffed calamari

You should be able to buy calamari tubes ready to cook, but if not, ask your fishmonger to clean and prepare some calamari for you. Another good way to cook calamari is to cut it into rings, dip it in batter and deep-fry until crisp.

1. Heat half the oil and the butter in a large pan and sauté the scallions, pepper, celery, and garlic for 5 minutes until soft but not browned.

2. Stir in the rice until hot, then add the wine and bring the boil. Boil for about 3 minutes until the wine has reduced.

3. Add the stock, tomato paste, cayenne, and parsley and bring to the boil. Turn down the heat, cover, and simmer gently for about 5 minutes until the rice is just tender and the liquid has been absorbed. Stir to make sure the rice does not stick to the pan. If it does, add a little boiling water.

4. Season with salt and pepper and remove from the heat. Leave to cool slightly.

5. Heat the oven to 180°C/350°F/Gas 4.

6. Fill the calamari tubes with the stuffing, securing the ends with toothpicks. Drizzle the remaining oil over the base of an ovenproof dish just large enough to hold the calamari. Place the stuffed calamari in the dish, turning to coat in the oil. Any remaining stuffing can be spooned around the calamari.

7. Cook in the oven for about 1 hour until tender and lightly browned on top. Garnish with rosemary and serve with the tomato sauce and a green salad.

Garlic pizza with arugula and olives

The Italians love their pizzas thin and crisp, often with the simplest of toppings. Here is the perfect pizza dough to top with your favorite ingredients. If you don't have a food processor, knead the dough by hand for 5–10 minutes.

Serves 4

For the pizza base

350g/12oz/3 cups bread flour

1½ tsp instant dried yeast

1 tsp sugar

A pinch of salt

2 tbsp olive oil

250ml/8fl oz/1 cup warm water

For the topping

6 garlic cloves, crushed

120ml/4fl oz/½ cup olive oil

Salt and freshly ground black pepper

100ml/3½fl oz/scant ½ cup sieved tomatoes (optional)

100g/4oz/¾ cup black olives, pitted

A few flatleaf parsley sprigs

100g/4oz arugula

To serve

A few vine tomatoes

1. Put the flour in a food processor and mix in the yeast, sugar, and salt. Add the oil. Gradually pour in the water with the processor running until you have a smooth dough; you may not need all the water. Continue to process for a few minutes so the dough is soft, elastic, and not sticky.
2. Wrap in plastic wrap and leave in a warm place for a couple of hours if you can; this will give you a lighter base.
3. Heat the oven to 200°C/400°F/Gas 6 and grease 2 large baking trays.
4. On a lightly floured surface, knock back the dough and divide in half. Roll out into 2 large thin rectangles to fit the baking trays and place on the trays.
5. Sprinkle with the garlic and drizzle with as much of the olive oil as you like. Season generously with salt and pepper. Spread the sieved tomatoes on top, if using, then chop half the olives and sprinkle on the top.
6. Bake in the hot oven for about 10 minutes until the base is cooked and the top is golden.
7. Sprinkle with the parsley, cut into wedges, and top with the arugula and the remaining olives. Serve with the vine tomatoes.

Bacon-wrapped chicken

Serves 4

4 chicken breasts

125g/4½oz/1 ball mozzarella, cut
　into 8 slices

8 large sage leaves

8 slices prosciutto crudo

1 tbsp olive oil

15g/½oz/1 tbsp butter

1 red bell pepper, cut into strips

1 yellow bell pepper, cut into strips

150ml/¼pt/⅔ cup white wine

Salt and freshly ground black pepper

350g/12oz macaroni

4 sage sprigs, to garnish

This is a simple but very impressive dish that you can serve for an evening meal or as a delicious dinner-party dish. If you prefer, you can also make it with veal escalopes or even turkey steaks.

1. Slice the chicken breasts in half horizontally. Place a slice of mozzarella and a sage leaf on each one and wrap in a slice of prosciutto, securing with a toothpick.

2. Heat the oil and butter in a shallow skillet and sauté the chicken over a high heat for a few minutes until just browned on both sides.

3. Reduce the heat, add the peppers, and sauté for a few minutes until they begin to soften.

4. Add the wine, bring to a simmer, partially cover and simmer for about 15 minutes until the chicken is cooked through.

5. Meanwhile, bring a large pan of lightly salted water to the boil, add the macaroni and boil for about 8 minutes until *al dente*. Take a bite to test whether it is ready.

6. Remove the lid from the chicken, raise the heat and cook quickly for a few minutes until most of the liquid has boiled away. Taste and season with pepper and a little salt if necessary.

7. Drain the pasta and spoon on to serving plates. Place the chicken on top, spoon the peppers over, and garnish with sage sprigs to serve.

Chicken cacciatore

This is a rich and flavorsome dish that you can cook in the oven or on the hob. It is most economical to buy a whole chicken and cut it into joints, or you can use chicken thighs, portions, or even diced chicken.

Serves 4

2 tbsp olive oil

12 chicken thighs

2 slices of bacon, rinded and chopped

2 onions, thinly sliced

2 garlic cloves, chopped

1 red bell pepper, sliced

1 green bell pepper, sliced

100g/4oz mushrooms, sliced

1 tsp dried oregano

150ml/¼pt/⅔ cup red wine

400g/14oz/1 large can chopped tomatoes

2 tbsp tomato paste

50g/2oz black olives, pitted

About 300ml/½pt/1¼ cups chicken stock

Salt and freshly ground black pepper

A few flatleaf parsley sprigs

1. Heat the oil in a large skillet or flameproof Dutch oven over a high heat and sauté the chicken until browned on all sides.
2. Reduce the heat, add the bacon, onions, garlic, and peppers, and sauté for a few minutes until soft but not browned.
3. Add the mushrooms and oregano and stir together well. Pour in the wine, bring to the boil, and simmer for 3 minutes.
4. Add the tomatoes, tomato paste, and olives, and enough of the stock to come just over halfway up the vegetables. Bring to a simmer, then simmer for about 30 minutes until the chicken is tender and the sauce is rich and thick.
5. Taste and season with salt and pepper and serve garnished with parsley.

Breaded pork with lemon

Pork with fruit is a popular combination because the fruit—especially a citrus fruit as in this recipe—counterbalances the richness of the pork. Leftover breadcrumbs can be dried in the oven, then stored in an airtight jar.

Serves 4

6 slices of stale bread
1 lemon
½ tsp paprika
Salt and freshly ground black pepper
1 tbsp all-purpose flour
1 egg, lightly beaten
4 thin pork sirloin cutlets
15g/½oz/1 tbsp butter
2 tbsp oil
4 savory sprigs

1. Heat the oven to 150°C/300°F/Gas 2.
2. Switch on a food processor or blender and drop pieces of the bread on to the rotating blades to whizz to a crumb. Spread the crumbs out on a cookie sheet and dry out in the oven for 5 minutes, watching carefully to make sure they go slightly golden and not too dark.
3. Meanwhile, cut the lemon in half. Cut one half into wedges. Grate the zest and squeeze the juice of the other half.
4. Remove the breadcrumbs from the oven and leave to cool slightly, then process again until very fine, adding the paprika and grated lemon zest and seasoning with salt and pepper.
5. Place the breadcrumbs, flour, and egg in separate shallow dishes. Dip the meat into the flour, then the egg, then the breadcrumbs, making sure it is well coated.
6. Heat the butter and oil in a large skillet, add the pork, and cook for about 5 minutes each side, turning a few times during cooking, until the pork is tender and the breadcrumbs are golden.
7. Sprinkle with the lemon juice, then served garnished with the savory sprig and the lemon wedges.

Lasagne

The archetypal Italian meal, this involves long, slow cooking so it is reserved for special meals. The longer you cook the ragù, the better it will taste.

Serves 4

For the ragù

2 tbsp olive oil
1 onion, finely chopped
1 carrot, diced
1 celery stick, diced
1 bay leaf
2 garlic cloves, finely chopped
500g/1lb ground beef
120ml/4fl oz/½ cup red wine
400g/14oz/1 large can chopped tomatoes
2 tbsp tomato paste
1 tsp dried oregano
Salt and freshly ground black pepper
400g/14oz lasagne sheets
50g/2oz/½ cup freshly grated Parmesan cheese
1 basil sprig

For the béchamel sauce

4 cloves
1 onion, halved
750ml/1¼pt/3 cups milk
4 black peppercorns
1 bay leaf
50g/2oz/¼ cup butter
50g/2oz/½ cup all-purpose flour

To finish

8–10 lasagne sheets
Ciabatta
Mixed green salad

1. Heat the olive oil in a pan and sauté the onion, carrot, celery, and bay leaf, stirring occasionally, for 5 minutes until softened. Add the garlic and continue to sauté for 3 minutes, stirring occasionally.
2. Add the beef and stir until browned and the grains are separate.
3. Add the wine, increase the heat, and cook until most of the liquid has evaporated.
4. Stir in the tomatoes, tomato paste, and oregano, and season with salt and pepper. Reduce the heat and simmer gently for 1½ hours, stirring occasionally, until rich and thick.
5. Meanwhile, make the béchamel sauce. Press the cloves into the onion and put in a pan with the milk, peppercorns and bay leaf. Bring to the boil, then remove from the heat, place a sheet of waxed paper on the surface and leave the milk to stand and infuse until the meat is almost cooked.
6. Heat the oven to 200°C/400°F/Gas 6.
7. Melt the butter in a large pan, then whisk in the flour and cook over a low heat for 2 minutes. Strain the milk into the pan and bring to the boil, whisking until thickened. Simmer gently for 5 minutes, stirring occasionally. Season to taste with salt and pepper.
8. Place the lasagne sheets in a colander and rinse with boiling water.
9. Spoon a layer of the meat over the base of a large ovenproof dish, then place some lasagne sheets on top, then a spoonful of the béchamel sauce. Continue to layer in this way until you have used all the ingredients, finishing with a layer of sauce. Sprinkle with the Parmesan cheese and an extra grating of black pepper. Bake in the oven for 40–45 minutes until golden brown.
10. Garnish with the basil and serve with ciabatta and a mixed green salad.

Serves 4

For the meatballs

600g/1lb 6oz ground beef

2 slices bacon, rinded and chopped

1 onion, chopped

1 garlic clove, chopped

60g/3oz/1 cup fresh breadcrumbs

2 tsp dried oregano

25g/1oz/¼ cup freshly grated
Parmesan cheese

Salt and freshly ground black pepper

30g/1oz/2 tbsp flour

1 tbsp olive oil

300ml/½pt/1¼ cups Tomato Sauce (page 22)

For the pasta

350g/12oz spaghetti

To serve

2 tbsp freshly grated Parmesan cheese

A few flatleaf parsley sprigs

Spaghetti and meatballs

Including the Parmesan and bacon in the mixture makes these meatballs really rich and tasty once all the flavors have blended together. You can use basil instead of oregano in the meatballs if you prefer, in which case, garnish with a little more fresh basil.

1. Mix the beef with the bacon, onion, garlic, breadcrumbs, oregano, and Parmesan. Season with pepper (you shouldn't need salt if you include bacon). Shape into balls—you can make them any size you like. Roll them in flour, shaking off the excess.

2. Heat the oil in a skillet and sauté the meatballs over a medium heat, turning frequently, until cooked through and browned on the outside, draining off the fat during cooking, if necessary.

3. While they are cooking, bring a large pan of salted water to the boil. Add the spaghetti and boil for about 5 minutes until the spaghetti is *al dente*.

4. When the meatballs are browned, pour in the tomato sauce and bring to a simmer. Check and adjust the seasoning to taste.

5. Drain the spaghetti well and serve on to plates. Spoon the meatballs and sauce over, sprinkle with the Parmesan, and garnish with the parsley.

Fried risotto balls

Arancini di riso, or 'little rice oranges', are a Sicilian street food, delicious hot or cold, as a snack or appetizer, or for lunch with fresh salad. If you don't have any leftover cooked risotto, either make some (see page 23) or simply cook some risotto rice in chicken or vegetable stock.

Serves 4

400g/14oz cooked risotto, chilled
250g/9oz/2 balls of mozzarella
Salt and freshly ground black pepper
30g/1oz/2 tbsp all-purpose flour
2 eggs, lightly beaten
100g/4oz/2 cups fine fresh breadcrumbs
120ml/4fl oz/½ cup olive oil

1. Cold risotto will hold together better, so make sure the risotto is well chilled. With lightly floured hands, shape the risotto into an even number of small balls, about the size of golf balls (although you can make them larger if you wish). Press your thumb into each one to shape it into a semi-sphere.

2. Cut the mozzarella into chunks, one for each hollowed risotto ball, and press a piece of mozzarella into each hole, then mold 2 together to encase the cheese in the rice. Repeat until you have pressed them all into pairs.

3. Put the flour, egg, and breadcrumbs in 3 separate shallow bowls. Roll the balls in the flour, then the egg, and finally the breadcrumbs.

4. Heat enough of the oil in a large, shallow pan to cover the base. Add the risotto balls to the hot oil, in batches if necessary, and sauté for about 5–6 minutes, turning until golden on all sides and piping hot.

5. Serve the risotto balls either on their own or with salad.

Potato gnocchi with tomato sauce

Serves 4

For the gnocchi

450g/1lb floury potatoes, peeled and cut into chunks

30g/1oz/2 tbsp butter

Salt and freshly ground black pepper

75g/3oz/¾ cup plain flour, plus more for dusting

1 egg yolk

For the sauce

1 tbsp olive oil

1 onion, finely chopped

1–2 garlic cloves, finely chopped

1 celery stick, finely chopped

1 carrot, finely chopped

400g/14oz/1 large can chopped tomatoes

2 tbsp tomato paste

2 tsp oregano

50g/2oz/½ cup freshly grated Parmesan cheese

A few basil sprigs

You can buy potato gnocchi for a quick and tasty meal but it's much more satisfying to make your own. This versatile tomato sauce can be used for pasta, pizza toppings, and all kinds of Italian dishes.

1. Put the potatoes in a pan of salted water, bring to the boil, and simmer for about 10 minutes until soft, then drain.
2. Mash with the butter and season with salt and pepper. Stir in the flour and egg yolk and mix to a fairly stiff dough.
3. On a lightly floured surface, roll the dough into a long sausage shape and cut off 2.5cm/1in lengths. Press a pattern on each of the gnocchi with a fork, dipped in flour so that it doesn't stick.
4. To make the tomato sauce, heat the oil and sauté the onion, garlic, celery, and carrot for about 5 minutes until soft but not browned.
5. Add the tomatoes, tomato paste, and oregano, and leave to simmer gently for at least 10 minutes, preferably 30 minutes. Season to taste with salt and pepper.
6. Use it as it is for a chunky sauce, purée for a thick sauce, or purée then rub through a sieve for a fine sauce.
7. While the sauce is cooking, bring a large pan of salted water to the boil. Add some of the gnocchi and boil for about 2 minutes until they rise to the surface. Lift out with a slotted spoon, drain thoroughly and keep them warm while you return the water to the boil and cook the remaining gnocchi.
8. Spoon the sauce over the gnocchi, sprinkle generously with the Parmesan, and serve garnished with basil.

There are several kinds of risotto rice, the most common being arborio and carnaroli. They all have their own qualities so try different ones to see which you prefer. They are a medium-grain rice that give a lovely, creamy result.

Wild mushroom risotto

Serves 4

25g/1oz dried porcini mushrooms
2 tbsp olive oil
1 onion, finely chopped
2 garlic cloves, chopped
2 scallions, finely chopped
350g/12oz/1⅔ cups arborio or other risotto rice
150ml/¼pt/⅔ cup white wine
150g/6oz mushrooms, thinly sliced
A pinch of saffron strands
1.2 litres/2 pts/5 cups hot vegetable stock
Salt and freshly ground black pepper
100g/4oz/1 cup freshly grated Parmesan cheese
2 tbsp crème fraîche

1. Pour boiling water over the dried mushrooms and leave to soak for 30 minutes. Strain, reserving a little of the soaking liquid. Strain the liquid through a fine sieve.
2. In a large pan, heat the oil and sauté the onion and garlic gently until soft but not browned. Add most of the scallions, reserving a few green pieces.
3. Add the rice and stir until hot and coated in oil. Add the wine and bring to a simmer. Add the fresh mushrooms and saffron, then the strained dried mushrooms.
4. Start adding the hot stock a little at a time, stirring until it has been absorbed before adding more. Continue in this way until the rice is cooked and creamy but still *al dente*. This will take about 20 minutes.
5. Remove from the heat. Season with salt and pepper and stir in most of the cheese and the crème fraîche. Cover and leave to stand for 2 minutes, then serve garnished with the reserved scallions and Parmesan.

Italian braised beef

Long, slow cooking produces the perfect results for this dish, giving succulent, tender meat coated in a rich and thick gravy. You can use peppers of various colors to liven up the dish.

Serves 4

3 tbsp olive oil
2 onions, sliced
2 garlic cloves, chopped
1 red bell pepper, chopped
1 orange bell pepper, sliced
225g/8oz mushrooms, halved or sliced
350g/12oz braising steak, cut into chunks
450g/1lb new potatoes
150ml/¼pt/⅔ cup red wine
300ml/½pt/1¼ cups beef stock
3 tbsp tomato paste
2 parsley sprigs, chopped
2 rosemary sprigs
Salt and freshly ground black pepper

To serve
Roast new potatoes

1. Heat the oven to 180°C/350°F/Gas 4.
2. Heat half the oil in a large sauté pan. Sauté the onions and garlic over a medium heat for a few minutes until soft but not browned. Add the peppers and sauté for 5 minutes. Add the mushrooms and sauté until soft, then spoon the contents of the pan into a casserole dish.
3. Turn up the heat and add the remaining oil. Add the steak to the pan and sauté, stirring, until browned on all sides. Spoon into the casserole dish.
4. Add the potatoes to the pan and sauté for a few minutes until golden, then transfer to the dish.
5. Pour the wine into the pan and bring to the boil, stirring. Add the stock and tomato paste and return to the boil. Pour over the ingredients in the casserole and add the parsley and a sprig of rosemary. Season to taste with salt and pepper.
6. Cover and cook in the oven for 40 minutes, then reduce the temperature to 160°C/325°F/Gas 3 for a further 2 hours until the meat is tender and the sauce is thick. Check the casserole occasionally and remove the lid towards the end of cooking if you need to reduce the liquid.
7. Garnish with a little more rosemary and serve with roasted potatoes.

Baked vegetable pasta

Pasta makes lovely baked dishes, this one combining macaroni and vegetables in a cheese sauce, which is then baked until just beginning to go golden on the top. You can make it in one large dish or individual dishes, to serve straight from the oven.

Serves 4

400g/14oz/4 cups macaroni or other pasta
Salt and freshly ground black pepper
100g/4oz small cauliflower florets
100g/4oz small broccoli florets
100g/4oz/1 cup freshly grated Parmesan cheese

For the sauce

15g/½oz/1 tbsp butter
1 tbsp olive oil
1 onion, finely chopped
1 garlic clove, chopped
1 red bell pepper, chopped
1 tbsp all-purpose flour
250ml/8fl oz/1 cup milk
250ml/8fl oz/1 cup chicken or vegetable stock

To serve
Fresh mixed salad

1. Heat the oven to 200°C/400°F/Gas 6.
2. Heat a large pan of lightly salted water, add the macaroni, and boil for about 8 minutes until the pasta is *al dente*. Add the cauliflower and broccoli, return to the boil, then drain immediately just to blanch the vegetables.
3. Meanwhile, heat the butter and oil in a skillet and sauté the onion, garlic, and pepper for a few minutes until soft but not browned.
4. Stir in the flour and cook for 1 minute, stirring continuously. Gradually whisk in the milk and stock and bring to a simmer, stirring until the sauce is smooth. Stir in half the Parmesan and season with salt and pepper.
5. Spoon the vegetables into an ovenproof dish and pour the sauce over. Sprinkle with the remaining Parmesan.
6. Bake in the oven for 20 minutes until golden. Serve with a fresh mixed salad.

Chicken and olive pasta

Pasta is the perfect partner to all kinds of sauces, making it very useful for all of us with a busy lifestyle. This light sauce makes for a moist and tasty coating to the pasta, and you can use any pasta shape you like.

Serves 4

350g/12oz linguine or other pasta
Salt and freshly ground black pepper
2 tbsp olive oil
1 garlic clove, chopped
350g/12oz chicken breasts, cut into small pieces
4 tomatoes, chopped
1 red bell pepper, finely chopped
120ml/4fl oz/½ cup white wine
120ml/4fl oz/½ cup chicken stock
100g/4oz black olives, pitted and halved
50g/2oz/½ cup finely grated Parmesan cheese (optional)
2 tbsp crème fraîche
A few flatleaf parsley sprigs

1. Bring a large pan of lightly salted water to the boil. Add the pasta and simmer gently for about 8 minutes until tender.
2. Meanwhile, heat the oil in a skillet and sauté the garlic and chicken for a few minutes until golden on all sides.
3. Add the tomatoes and pepper and continue to sauté until well blended. Add the wine and boil for 2 minutes. Add the stock and bring to a gentle simmer. Add the olives to the chicken and stir well. Stir in half the Parmesan cheese, if using.
4. Remove both pans from the heat. Drain the pasta and toss with the chicken. Stir in the crème fraîche, sprinkle with the remaining Parmesan, and serve garnished with the parsley.

Serves 4

4 eggs, separated

250g/9oz/1 tub mascarpone

60g/2oz/4 tbsp golden
superfine sugar

120ml/4fl oz/½ cup strong
coffee, cooled

75g/3oz/1 small bar dark
chocolate, chopped

4 tbsp Marsala
or brandy

175g/6oz/1 pack ladyfinger biscuits

1 tsp cocoa powder

1 tsp coffee granules

Tiramisù

This classic dessert is best made a day ahead of time and kept in the fridge for the flavors to infuse and mature. Cover tightly with plastic wrap and don't be tempted to take a spoonful—you'll never be able to stop at one!

1. Beat the egg whites until stiff and put to one side.
2. In a separate bowl, whisk the egg yolks until pale, then beat in the mascarpone, sugar, and 1 tbsp of the coffee until well blended. Fold in the egg whites, then the chocolate.
3. Put the remaining coffee in a shallow dish with the Marsala or brandy.
4. One at a time, dip half the ladyfingers into the coffee to soak up some of the mixture and arrange on the base of a serving dish. Spread with half the mascarpone mixture.
5. Dip the remaining ladyfingers to use up the liquid and arrange on top, then spoon the remaining mascarpone mixture over.
6. Put the cocoa and coffee granules in a fine sieve and sprinkle over the top.
7. Cover with plastic wrap, not allowing it to touch the tiramisù, and chill in the fridge, if possible, overnight or for up to 2 days before serving.

Cantuccini biscotti

Twice baked, these crisp almond biscotti are perfect to serve with afternoon coffee or to offer your guests at the end of a meal. Because they are crisped by slicing and baking the cut slices, they hold together when you dunk them in your hot coffee.

Makes about 16

100g/4oz/1 cup all-purpose flour
100g/4oz/1 cup ground almonds
1 tsp baking powder
A pinch of salt
50g/2oz/¼ cup butter, melted
1 tbsp Amaretto
1 tsp almond extract
2 eggs
225g/8oz/1 cup superfine sugar
75g/3oz/¾ cup almonds

1. Heat the oven to 180°C/350°F/Gas 4 and grease a cookie sheet.
2. Mix together the flour, almonds, baking powder, and salt. Stir in the melted butter, Amaretto, and almond extract.
3. Whisk the eggs and sugar until pale, then fold into the flour mixture. Gently stir in the almonds.
4. With lightly floured hands, shape the mixture into a broad roll about 25cm/10in long and place on the prepared cookie sheet.
5. Bake in the oven for about 20 minutes until just golden.
6. Remove from the oven and reduce the oven temperature to 160°C/320°F/Gas 3. Cut the roll into thick slices, arrange them flat on the cookie sheet and return to the oven for about 5–10 minutes until golden.
7. Leave to cool on a wire rack.

Panna cotta

If you are serving this to guests, make it well ahead of time so that it has plenty of time to set. Choose your favorite summer fruit to make the coulis.

Serves 4

4 sheets of gelatin or 1 tsp powdered
  gelatin
600ml/1pt/2½ cups heavy cream
100g/4oz/½ cup superfine sugar
1 tsp vanilla extract

For the strawberry syrup
225g/8oz strawberries
225g/8oz raspberries
100g/4oz/½ cup superfine sugar
1 tbsp dash of orange liqueur (optional)

To garnish
A small mint sprig

1. Place the gelatin in a shallow bowl and just cover with cold water. If you have powdered gelatin, disolve 1 tsp in a little hot but not boiling water.
2. Put the cream and sugar in a saucepan over a low heat and stir gently until the sugar has dissolved, then bring to the boil. Remove from the heat.
3. If using gelatin leaves, squeeze out any excess water. Whisk the gelatin into the boiling mixture. Strain through a fine sieve, then leave to cool slightly.
4. Rinse 4 individual molds or teacups with water, then pour the mixture in and chill in the fridge for at least 2 hours until set.
5. To make the strawberry syrup, reserve a few strawberries and raspberries for decoration. Put the rest in a pan with the sugar and the liqueur, if using, and bring slowly to a simmer, crushing the berries into the syrup.
6. Strain to achieve a smooth syrup, or leave the seeds in if you prefer. Leave to cool.
7. Turn out the panna cotta on to serving plates, dipping the molds briefly in hot water to loosen them from the molds. Pour the syrup over and garnish.